JADEN CROSS

API Gateway Design Patterns For Cloud Computing

Contents

Foundations of API Gateway Design

A PI gateways have become a foundational component in modern cloud-based architectures, transforming how businesses design and deploy applications. As businesses migrate from monolithic to microservices and serverless architectures, the role of API gateways has evolved significantly, bridging gaps in security, scalability, and ease of management. In this section, we'll delve into the fundamentals of API gateway design, their importance in cloud computing, and key trends shaping their usage today.

What is an API Gateway?

An API gateway is an architectural component that serves as an entry point for all client requests. Think of it as the receptionist at the front desk of a large corporation, managing all interactions between external clients and internal services. Its primary function is to receive API calls, route them to the appropriate microservices, and return responses to clients.

Traditionally, applications relied on direct communication between the client and server. However, as organizations adopted cloud computing and broke monolithic applications into smaller, independent services, the complexity of managing multiple APIs increased. Enter the API gateway: a solution to centralize request routing, enhance security, streamline monitoring, and ensure consistency across services.

Some of the essential responsibilities of an API gateway include:

- **Request Routing**: Directing incoming API requests to the appropriate microservices.

- **Rate Limiting and Throttling**: Managing the number of requests received within a specified timeframe to protect backend services from overloading.
- **Security**: Authenticating and authorizing users and traffic, ensuring only legitimate requests reach the services.
- **Load Balancing**: Distributing incoming requests across different instances of microservices to enhance system reliability.
- **Caching**: Reducing latency by storing frequently accessed data and reducing redundant backend service calls.

Evolution of API Management in Cloud Computing

API management has transformed over the years, evolving from basic reverse proxies to sophisticated gateways capable of handling complex architectural requirements. Initially, applications operated as monolithic entities—single, massive structures. Scaling and maintaining such architectures was challenging, leading to a shift towards microservices and, subsequently, cloud-native applications.

This shift required new approaches to handle the increased number of services, each responsible for a discrete function. API gateways emerged as a necessary abstraction layer, simplifying communication, security, and governance between these services.

The Rise of Microservices and Cloud-Native Architectures: With microservices, different components of an application can scale independently and be managed by separate teams. This change required a central mechanism to coordinate service-to-service communication while maintaining consistency in authentication, logging, and traffic management. Cloud platforms like AWS, Azure, and Google Cloud offered API gateways to fulfill these needs.

Serverless Architecture and the Role of API Gateways: In serverless architectures, API gateways play a critical role in bridging client requests to functions like AWS Lambda or Azure Functions. By serving as a central endpoint, API gateways simplify the routing and orchestration of serverless workflows, allowing developers to focus on function implementation rather than managing infrastructure.

Key Roles of an API Gateway in Modern Architectures

API gateways aren't merely traffic controllers. They play crucial roles in modern cloud-based systems, providing essential functionalities to ensure robust, scalable, and secure architectures. Below are some of the key responsibilities that API gateways fulfill:

1. **Centralized Security Enforcement**: As a single entry point for all external requests, API gateways enforce security measures like rate limiting, OAuth2, JWT validation, and IP filtering. This centralization ensures that all services behind the gateway are shielded from direct exposure to potentially malicious traffic.

2. **Traffic Management and Load Balancing**: API gateways manage traffic distribution to different instances of a microservice. This not only prevents overloading of specific instances but also allows for optimized resource utilization.

3. **Service Discovery**: In dynamic environments where services can scale up or down automatically, API gateways often integrate with service registries to dynamically route requests to active service instances.

4. **Cross-Cutting Concerns Management**: API gateways centralize functions like logging, monitoring, caching, and authentication, which otherwise would have to be implemented individually across services. This results in simplified codebases and a unified architecture.

5. **Protocol Translation**: In many scenarios, API gateways are responsible for translating protocols (e.g., from HTTP to gRPC or WebSocket), making it easier to integrate diverse systems and clients.

Current Trends and Challenges in API Management

As cloud computing matures, the importance of API gateways continues to grow. They are not static components; instead, they evolve alongside advancements in microservices, security, and cloud-native solutions. In this

3

section, we will explore some key trends and challenges affecting the use of API gateways:

1. **Multi-Cloud and Hybrid Architectures**: Organizations are increasingly adopting multi-cloud strategies to avoid vendor lock-in and enhance resilience. This trend requires API gateways to support seamless integration and routing across different cloud platforms. API gateways must enable consistent security policies and provide unified management, regardless of where the services reside.

2. **Zero Trust Security**: With cyber threats on the rise, zero trust architecture is gaining traction. API gateways are playing an essential role in implementing zero trust models, focusing on verifying each request regardless of its origin. Zero trust requires continuous monitoring and assessment of all traffic passing through the API gateway, enforcing strict identity and access controls.

3. **Edge Computing**: As businesses push services closer to users, edge computing has introduced new challenges for API management. API gateways need to support hybrid environments that combine cloud and edge infrastructure. This trend also demands real-time synchronization between centralized and edge-deployed API gateways.

4. **API Monetization and Developer Portals**: Monetization of APIs is becoming common, especially among SaaS providers. API gateways are evolving to facilitate metering, monetization, and exposure of APIs through developer portals, allowing businesses to provide secure and efficient access to third-party developers.

5. **Adoption of GraphQL and gRPC**: With traditional REST APIs showing limitations in flexibility, the adoption of GraphQL and gRPC is growing. API gateways are required to adapt to these newer protocols, offering features like schema stitching, request validation, and translation between GraphQL and RESTful endpoints.

Despite these advancements, several challenges persist in API management. One significant challenge is **performance optimization**, as gateways introduce additional latency. Addressing scalability, fault tolerance, and efficient caching mechanisms are critical to overcoming this. Additionally, **managing distributed services** behind an API gateway can be complex, requiring robust observability, monitoring, and tracing tools.

Real-World Case Studies from Leading Cloud Providers

To better understand the role and implementation of API gateways, let's explore some real-world examples from leading cloud providers:

AWS API Gateway: In AWS, the API Gateway serves as a fully managed service, capable of handling thousands of concurrent API requests and connecting them to AWS Lambda functions, EC2 instances, and other AWS services. AWS API Gateway offers powerful features such as caching, WebSocket support, and integrated OAuth2, making it a versatile choice for serverless and microservices-based applications.

Case Study Example: A fintech company uses AWS API Gateway to provide secure and scalable API access to its mobile banking app. The gateway ensures security with JWT-based authentication, rate limits to prevent abuse, and API caching to reduce latency. The backend, built on Lambda functions, handles transaction processing, while the API Gateway manages all client-facing traffic.

Azure API Management: Microsoft Azure's API Management service provides a unified API gateway to publish, secure, and monitor APIs. It includes built-in support for exposing APIs from Azure-based and on-premises services and supports seamless integration with Azure Active Directory for enterprise authentication needs.

Case Study Example: A healthcare provider uses Azure API Management to expose APIs for patient data access to external partners. With the API Management service, the healthcare provider enforces strict access controls, maintains compliance with HIPAA regulations, and monitors traffic using Azure's analytics tools. By centralizing API management, the provider ensures consistent security and scalability.

Google Cloud Apigee: Apigee, part of Google Cloud, offers a highly flexible and enterprise-grade API management solution. It provides advanced features like API monetization, usage reporting, OAuth2 and SAML integration, and seamless integration with Kubernetes and Istio for service mesh implementations.

Case Study Example: A media company leverages Apigee to offer APIs for accessing video content to external developers. By using Apigee's API monetization features, the company charges partners based on API usage. Apigee handles all aspects of security, versioning, and API analytics, freeing the company to focus on content delivery and user experience.

These case studies highlight the varied capabilities and applications of API gateways across different industries. Depending on their needs, organizations can select a cloud provider's built-in solution or deploy third-party options like Kong, NGINX, or Tyk.

API Gateway vs Reverse Proxy vs Load Balancer

One common point of confusion in API management is the distinction between an API gateway, a reverse proxy, and a load balancer. Although these components share some functionalities, they serve different roles within a cloud architecture:

- **API Gateway**: A central component in microservices architecture, managing external client interactions, providing cross-cutting functionalities, and serving as the central entry point for all API requests. API gateways focus on handling API-level functionalities such as security, routing, monitoring, and protocol translation.
- **Reverse Proxy**: Primarily used to forward client requests to backend servers. It improves performance, offers SSL termination, and provides a layer of security by obscuring backend services from direct exposure. Reverse proxies lack the full-fledged API management capabilities of an API gateway.
- **Load Balancer**: A load balancer's core function is to distribute incoming traffic across multiple server instances based on various algorithms (e.g.,

round-robin, least connections). It focuses purely on load distribution and failover management.

While the differences may seem subtle, the choice between these components depends on the specific requirements of an architecture. In many cases, API gateways include reverse proxy and load balancing functionalities, simplifying deployment and maintenance.

Essential Design Patterns for API Gateways

D esign patterns are crucial for creating scalable, secure, and
resilient architectures. They provide repeatable solutions for
common problems and help developers implement best practices
consistently. In the context of API gateways, design patterns not only help in
managing traffic and services but also in optimizing security, performance,
and flexibility. This section explores the essential design patterns for API
gateways, focusing on how each pattern addresses specific challenges in
cloud-native architectures.

Backend-for-Frontend (BFF) Pattern

The **Backend-for-Frontend (BFF)** pattern is a crucial design approach
used in API gateway architecture. In essence, the BFF pattern involves
creating separate backend services tailored to the specific needs of each user
interface or client application. Instead of a single generic backend, each client
gets a dedicated backend that understands its requirements and provides only
the data and logic it needs.

Why Use the BFF Pattern?

In traditional monolithic applications, there is usually one backend serving
all types of clients—web, mobile, and third-party applications. However, each
of these clients often has distinct requirements in terms of data, functionality,
and user experience. For instance, a mobile app might require lighter payloads
due to bandwidth constraints, while a web application might benefit from

larger data sets and more detailed information.

The BFF pattern solves this issue by introducing a dedicated API gateway or backend for each client. This approach leads to:

- **Optimized Data Transfer**: Each client only receives the data it needs, reducing unnecessary payloads and bandwidth consumption.
- **Client-Specific Logic**: Business logic specific to each client is handled separately, resulting in cleaner and more manageable codebases.
- **Decoupling of Frontend and Backend**: Allows teams to work independently on client-side features without affecting other clients.

Implementing the BFF Pattern

Let's consider a real-world example of an eCommerce platform with a web application and a mobile app. The web application provides a rich user experience with multiple filters, detailed product descriptions, and additional recommendation sections. In contrast, the mobile app offers a simplified view to prioritize speed and usability on small screens.

Using the BFF pattern, you would create two distinct API gateways:

1. **Web BFF Gateway**: Manages the routes and logic for web clients, delivering comprehensive data and additional UI-centric elements.
2. **Mobile BFF Gateway**: Manages the routes and logic for mobile clients, optimizing payload sizes and providing concise, mobile-friendly data.

In terms of implementation, each BFF gateway can be built using cloud-specific API management solutions such as AWS API Gateway, Azure API Management, or open-source tools like Kong. They can also connect to separate microservices or orchestrate multiple services behind the scenes.

The following diagram illustrates how the BFF pattern works:

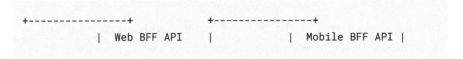

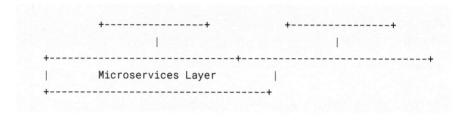

```
      +---------------+           +----------------+
      |               |           |                |
 +-------------------------------+----------------------------+
 |            Microservices Layer              |
 +---------------------------------------------+
```

The key advantage of this pattern is the ability to independently scale, modify, and enhance each backend as per the specific client requirements. Additionally, it reduces the risk of introducing breaking changes that could affect other clients, improving the overall maintainability of the application.

Microservices Proxy Pattern

In modern architectures, applications are often composed of numerous microservices, each focusing on a single, well-defined responsibility. However, managing these microservices individually can become complex, especially when dealing with service-to-service communication, security policies, and routing.

The **Microservices Proxy Pattern** involves using an API gateway as an intermediary that manages and routes traffic between microservices. The primary objective of this pattern is to abstract the complexity of individual microservices from external clients, providing a unified interface for communication.

Benefits of the Microservices Proxy Pattern

- **Simplified Routing**: Instead of exposing each microservice to external clients, the API gateway provides a single endpoint that intelligently routes requests.
- **Centralized Security**: Security features like authentication, authorization, and SSL termination are handled at the gateway level, preventing unauthorized access to internal services.
- **Reduced Client Complexity**: Clients interact with a unified API, abstracting the complexity of microservices behind the gateway.

Implementation Example

Suppose you are developing a content delivery platform with separate microservices for video streaming, user management, and analytics. Exposing these microservices directly to the frontend introduces several challenges, including coordinating security policies, managing API versions, and handling rate limits.

In this case, implementing the Microservices Proxy Pattern allows you to achieve the following:

- **Centralized Entry Point**: The API gateway serves as the entry point for all client interactions. It intelligently routes requests to the appropriate microservices based on configured paths.
- **Centralized Security and Monitoring**: Authentication, rate limiting, logging, and monitoring are implemented at the gateway level, reducing complexity within each microservice.

The following diagram illustrates the architecture:

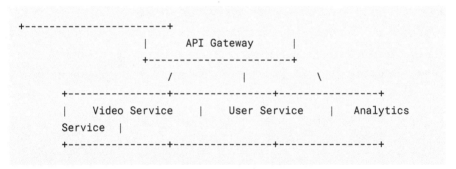

```
+----------------------+
|     API Gateway      |
+----------------------+
     /         |         \
+---------------+---------------+---------------+
|  Video Service |  User Service | Analytics
 Service |
+---------------+---------------+---------------+
```

In this approach, the API gateway is responsible for receiving requests, performing authentication, routing traffic, and even transforming responses if necessary. This setup significantly reduces the burden on individual microservices, allowing them to focus purely on business logic.

Edge Service Pattern

The **Edge Service Pattern** positions the API gateway at the edge of your network to serve as the first line of defense against external threats and to handle essential services like SSL termination, API rate limiting, and filtering. This pattern is particularly useful for applications that expose public-facing APIs, as it secures the gateway and reduces the attack surface for internal services.

Key Characteristics of the Edge Service Pattern

- **SSL Termination**: The API gateway handles SSL/TLS decryption and encryption, offloading this responsibility from backend services. This centralizes encryption policies and reduces resource consumption for internal microservices.
- **Traffic Filtering**: The gateway filters incoming traffic based on security rules, IP blacklists, and other policies to prevent malicious requests from reaching backend services.
- **Request Validation and Normalization**: It validates request payloads, headers, and authentication tokens to ensure that only well-formed and authorized requests reach backend systems.

Example Use Case: A Financial Services Platform

In a financial services platform, multiple services like account management, transaction processing, and loan services interact with external clients. Given the sensitivity of financial data, it is crucial to implement stringent security measures at the gateway level.

An API gateway deployed as an edge service would handle the following responsibilities:

- **SSL Termination**: Decrypt incoming SSL traffic to inspect request headers and payloads, ensuring secure communication.
- **Request Throttling and DDoS Mitigation**: Protect backend services by rate limiting excessive requests and blocking suspected DDoS attempts.
- **Authentication and Authorization**: Enforce multi-factor authentication and JWT validation to confirm that only authorized users can access financial services.

Strangler Fig Pattern for Legacy Migration

When transitioning from monolithic to microservices architecture, a common challenge is the risk of disrupting existing functionality. The **Strangler Fig Pattern** offers a solution by gradually replacing components of a monolithic system with new microservices, using an API gateway to route traffic between the old and new systems during the transition.

Key Features of the Strangler Fig Pattern

- **Incremental Migration**: Allows for gradual migration of features and components, reducing risk and enabling continuous deployment.
- **Fallback to Legacy**: During the transition, requests can be selectively routed to either the new microservices or the legacy system, ensuring smooth operation and minimal downtime.
- **Unified Client Interaction**: From the client's perspective, there is no difference between old and new services. The API gateway abstracts the details of routing and feature migration.

Implementation Example

Suppose you are migrating a monolithic eCommerce application to a microservices-based architecture. The application handles multiple features like product catalog, payment processing, and order management. Instead of rewriting the entire application, the Strangler Fig Pattern enables you to implement microservices for individual features incrementally.

1. **Step 1: Deploy the API Gateway**: Introduce an API gateway that acts as the entry point for all client requests.
2. **Step 2: Implement the First Microservice**: Develop and deploy a microservice for a feature like the product catalog. Configure the API gateway to route requests related to the catalog to this new microservice.
3. **Step 3: Migrate Additional Features**: Gradually replace other features like payment processing and order management with microservices. Update the API gateway's routing logic to direct requests accordingly.

This gradual migration approach minimizes risks and allows for continuous feature releases without significant downtime or client disruption.

Security Design Patterns

Security is a critical aspect of API gateway design. Implementing robust security measures at the gateway level ensures the protection of sensitive data and prevents unauthorized access. Several security-focused design patterns are commonly used with API gateways:

1. **Zero Trust Security**: API gateways play a vital role in implementing zero trust architectures by verifying every request regardless of its origin. This pattern focuses on identity verification, authorization, and continuous monitoring to ensure that only legitimate traffic reaches backend services.
2. **OAuth2 and JWT Integration**: Many organizations leverage API gateways to enforce OAuth2 authentication and JWT-based authorization. This allows for secure access control and token-based session management.
3. **TLS Termination and Encryption**: API gateways often handle TLS termination, providing a single point for SSL decryption and offloading the responsibility from individual services. Additionally, they can enforce policies for end-to-end encryption of sensitive data.
4. **Rate Limiting and Traffic Shaping**: API gateways implement rate limiting and traffic shaping policies to prevent abuse and denial-of-service (DoS) attacks. This is particularly crucial for public-facing APIs that are subject to varying traffic patterns.

Case Study: Implementing OAuth2 and Zero Trust with an API Gateway

In a healthcare application that handles patient data, implementing robust security is paramount. The application's architecture involves multiple microservices for appointment scheduling, patient records, and billing. By employing an API gateway with security-focused design patterns, the application achieves the following:

- **OAuth2 Authentication**: The API gateway acts as the OAuth2 authorization server, issuing JWTs to authenticated clients and validating these tokens with each request.
- **Zero Trust Security**: The gateway enforces identity verification and continuous monitoring, ensuring that even internal services communicate securely and verify the authenticity of each interaction.

Advanced API Gateway Implementations

As cloud computing evolves, the demands on API gateways are increasing. Beyond fundamental functionalities like routing, security, and load balancing, API gateways must now handle more sophisticated tasks such as multi-cloud integration, serverless management, and advanced monitoring. This section focuses on implementing advanced features using API gateways to create scalable, secure, and resilient cloud-native architectures.

Comparing Leading Cloud API Gateways

When choosing an API gateway solution, understanding the core features and benefits of various providers is critical. The three leading cloud providers—AWS, Azure, and Google Cloud—offer robust API gateway solutions: **AWS API Gateway**, **Azure API Management**, and **Google Cloud Apigee**. Let's delve into the distinguishing features, strengths, and optimal use cases for each.

AWS API Gateway

AWS API Gateway is a fully managed service that allows developers to create and manage REST, HTTP, and WebSocket APIs. It seamlessly integrates with other AWS services like Lambda, EC2, S3, and DynamoDB, making it an ideal choice for serverless and microservices architectures.

- **Key Features**:
- **Serverless Integration**: Tight integration with AWS Lambda allows for

direct execution of serverless functions.

- **Custom Authorizers**: Enables the use of Lambda functions to implement custom authentication logic.
- **Support for WebSocket APIs**: Allows the creation of real-time, two-way communication applications.
- **Stage Variables**: Facilitates environment-specific configurations, such as setting different database URIs for development and production.
- **Best Use Cases**:
- **Serverless Architectures**: For serverless-first strategies, AWS API Gateway combined with Lambda functions provides a cost-effective, scalable solution.
- **Low-Latency Applications**: Proximity to AWS's global infrastructure ensures low latency for applications.

Azure API Management

Azure API Management provides comprehensive API management capabilities, including publishing, securing, monitoring, and analyzing APIs. It is particularly strong in enterprises that already leverage Microsoft's suite of services and enterprise security solutions.

- **Key Features**:
- **Developer Portal**: Offers a customizable developer portal for exposing APIs to external or internal developers.
- **Policy-Based Configurations**: Allows for centralized implementation of security, caching, rate limiting, and other policies using a declarative format.
- **Hybrid and On-Premises Integration**: Supports API deployments in hybrid architectures, connecting on-premises systems to cloud-based APIs.
- **Best Use Cases**:
- **Enterprise Applications**: Perfect for enterprises leveraging Azure Active Directory for identity management and looking to expose APIs securely to internal or external stakeholders.

- **Hybrid Cloud Solutions**: Ideal for connecting on-premises data centers with Azure-based services.

Google Cloud Apigee

Apigee, part of Google Cloud, offers a full lifecycle API management platform with advanced features like API analytics, monetization, and traffic routing. Apigee's flexibility makes it a powerful option for organizations requiring in-depth control and detailed monitoring.

- **Key Features**:
- **API Monetization**: Provides tools for charging customers based on API usage with granular control.
- **Advanced Analytics and Reporting**: Offers real-time visibility into API traffic and usage patterns.
- **Microservices and Service Mesh Integration**: Integrates with Kubernetes and Istio for API management within service meshes.
- **Best Use Cases**:
- **Monetizing APIs**: Ideal for organizations looking to expose APIs as products and charge for their consumption.
- **Service Mesh Environments**: Suitable for managing APIs within Kubernetes clusters and implementing service mesh policies.

Key Features Comparison Table

The following table provides a side-by-side comparison of the key features of AWS API Gateway, Azure API Management, and Apigee:

Feature	AWS API Gateway	Azure API Management	Google Cloud Apigee
Serverless Integration	Tight integration with Lambda	Supports Azure Functions	Integrates with Cloud Functions
Custom Policies	Yes (via Lambda Authorizers)	Extensive built-in policies	Policy editor and flexible plugins
Real-Time APIs	Supports WebSocket APIs	Limited real-time support	Advanced WebSocket support
Developer Portal	Limited customization	Fully customizable portal	Feature-rich portal
Hybrid Cloud Support	Partial support (via VPC links)	Strong support for hybrid	Strong support (via Apigee hybrid)

End-to-End Project: Building an API Gateway from Scratch

Building an API gateway from scratch involves more than just deploying a service—it requires careful planning, consideration of client requirements, and configuration to meet business needs. In this project, we will walk through an end-to-end implementation of an API gateway for a hypothetical eCommerce platform using **AWS API Gateway**.

Project Overview

Scenario: We're designing an API gateway for an eCommerce platform called *CloudCart*. The platform offers multiple services like product browsing, order management, and payment processing. The primary goals for this gateway are to:

- Secure all APIs with OAuth2.
- Implement rate limiting to avoid abuse.
- Integrate with Lambda functions to handle business logic.

Step 1: Planning the Architecture
CloudCart's Requirements:

1. **User Authentication and Authorization**: All APIs must be protected using OAuth2 with JWT tokens.
2. **Efficient Routing**: Traffic should be routed to different Lambda

19

functions based on the requested path.

3. **Rate Limiting and Throttling**: Limit the number of requests to prevent abuse.

4. **API Versioning**: APIs should be versioned to handle future changes without disrupting existing services.

Proposed Architecture:

- **API Gateway** serves as the entry point for all incoming requests.
- **Cognito** handles user authentication and issues JWT tokens.
- **Lambda Functions** implement individual service logic for products, orders, and payments.
- **DynamoDB** is used for storing product and order data.

Step 2: Setting Up the API Gateway

- **Create an API Gateway in AWS Console**:
- Choose **REST API** and create a new gateway named *CloudCartAPI*.
- Define the root resource (/) and set up path-based routing for /products, /orders, and /payments.
- **Configure Authentication**:
- Create an Amazon Cognito user pool and define OAuth2 scopes for different levels of access (e.g., read:products, write:orders).
- Configure API Gateway to validate JWT tokens issued by Cognito. This can be done by setting up an authorizer in the **API Gateway Authorizer** section.
- **Define Rate Limiting**:
- Set up a usage plan with a **request quota** and **rate limit** (e.g., 1000 requests per user per day and 50 requests per second). Associate this plan with API keys that authorized users must present with each request.

Step 3: Implementing Business Logic with Lambda

For each API endpoint, define Lambda functions to handle incoming requests:

- **Products Service**: Lambda function fetches product details from DynamoDB.
- **Orders Service**: Lambda function validates and processes orders.
- **Payments Service**: Lambda function communicates with a payment gateway for transaction processing.

Configure API Gateway routes to invoke these Lambda functions based on the request path.

Step 4: Enforcing API Versioning

1. Create separate stages in API Gateway for each version (e.g., v1 and v2).
2. Route clients to different stages based on the version they request (e.g., /v1/products and /v2/products).
3. Use **Stage Variables** to manage environment-specific configurations like database URIs or feature toggles.

Step 5: Testing and Monitoring

1. **Testing**: Perform end-to-end testing for different scenarios such as authenticated and unauthenticated requests, rate-limited users, and valid versus invalid input data.
2. **Monitoring**: Enable AWS CloudWatch to track key metrics like request count, latency, error rates, and Lambda execution times. Set up alerts for critical issues like high error rates or request spikes.

Outcome and Benefits

By implementing this project, *CloudCart* gains the following benefits:

- **Enhanced Security**: JWT-based OAuth2 authentication ensures that only authorized users can access APIs.
- **Scalability**: API Gateway and Lambda functions automatically scale

based on traffic without manual intervention.

- **Fine-Grained Rate Limiting**: Usage plans and API keys help in controlling traffic and preventing abuse.

Integration Scenarios: Connecting APIs with Microservices and Legacy Systems

As organizations increasingly adopt microservices and serverless architectures, integrating these new systems with existing legacy applications becomes a significant challenge. In this section, we explore strategies for connecting APIs with both modern microservices and legacy monolithic systems using API gateways.

Scenario 1: Bridging Microservices and Monoliths

Problem Statement: A logistics company has a legacy monolithic application that handles order tracking and a new microservices architecture for route optimization. The goal is to connect these two systems using an API gateway while gradually migrating features to microservices.

Solution: Implement an API gateway that acts as an intermediary between the two systems:

- **Step 1: Expose Legacy APIs**: Create an API gateway that routes specific paths to the legacy application's endpoints.
- **Step 2: Introduce Microservices**: For features like route optimization, add new paths in the API gateway that forward traffic to dedicated microservices.
- **Step 3: Migrate Incrementally**: As new features are developed, gradually replace legacy endpoints with microservices. Update the API gateway's routing configuration to point to the new services.

Scenario 2: Integrating Serverless with Microservices

Problem Statement: A media streaming service uses microservices for content storage and delivery but wants to implement a recommendation engine using serverless functions.

Solution: Deploy an API gateway to connect microservices with serverless functions:

- **Step 1: Set Up the API Gateway**: Define routes for existing microservices and new serverless functions within the API gateway.
- **Step 2: Implement the Recommendation Engine**: Use serverless functions to analyze user data and generate content recommendations. The API gateway forwards requests from clients to this serverless function.
- **Step 3: Centralize Security and Logging**: Implement security policies and centralized logging at the gateway level to ensure consistency across serverless and microservices components.

Automation with CI/CD

To effectively manage and deploy API gateways, automating their configuration and deployment through Continuous Integration and Continuous Deployment (CI/CD) pipelines is crucial. Let's explore how to set up a CI/CD pipeline for API gateways using AWS CodePipeline:

1. **Define Infrastructure as Code (IaC)**: Use **AWS CloudFormation** or **Terraform** to define the API gateway configuration, Lambda functions, and DynamoDB tables as code. This ensures that infrastructure can be versioned, reviewed, and automatically deployed.
2. **Create a Build Pipeline**: Set up an AWS CodePipeline to automatically build and test Lambda functions. Use AWS CodeBuild for running unit tests and validating API definitions.
3. **Automate Deployment**: Upon successful testing, automatically deploy the API gateway configuration using the IaC templates. Implement manual approval steps for production deployments if required.

By automating the configuration and deployment of API gateways, organizations can achieve greater consistency, minimize human errors, and streamline the release process.

Optimizing and Monitoring API Gateways

O ptimizing and monitoring API gateways is essential to ensure high performance, reliability, and security for your applications. As the central entry point for all external traffic, an API gateway must efficiently route requests, maintain security policies, and handle high traffic loads without introducing latency or bottlenecks. In this section, we will explore performance optimization techniques, strategies for efficient monitoring, and ways to secure API gateways while maximizing their effectiveness in cloud-native architectures.

Performance Optimization Techniques

Performance is a key concern in API gateway implementation, as these gateways sit at the intersection of multiple services and handle all incoming requests. Poorly optimized gateways can introduce unnecessary latency, leading to a degraded user experience and increased costs.

1. API Caching Strategies for Improved Latency

Caching plays a crucial role in reducing latency and improving the responsiveness of APIs. API gateways can cache frequently accessed data, preventing the need to repeatedly query backend services for the same information. When implemented correctly, caching can significantly enhance performance and reduce backend load.

Key Considerations for Caching:

- **Data Granularity**: Determine what should be cached at the gateway level. For example, responses from static content APIs or frequently accessed catalog data can be cached.
- **Cache Invalidation**: Define strategies for cache invalidation to ensure that outdated or stale data isn't served to clients. API gateways can use time-based (TTL) or event-based cache invalidation mechanisms.
- **Request Headers and Query Parameters**: Consider how different request headers or query parameters affect cache keys. For example, user-specific data should not be cached globally.

Implementation Example: In AWS API Gateway, developers can enable caching for specific methods or endpoints and set TTL values. Using CloudFront as an additional caching layer in front of the API Gateway can further improve performance by caching responses at edge locations.

2. Handling High Traffic with Rate Limiting and Throttling

Rate limiting and throttling are essential features for managing high traffic loads and preventing abusive behavior. Rate limiting restricts the number of requests a client can make in a given timeframe, while throttling regulates request processing speeds to prevent backend overload.

Techniques for Effective Rate Limiting:

- **Quota-Based Rate Limiting**: Allocate a fixed number of requests to each client within a time window. For example, 1000 requests per day per user.
- **Dynamic Rate Limiting**: Adjust limits dynamically based on client behavior or request patterns, applying stricter limits on suspicious activity.
- **Throttling Policies**: Implement throttling to control the speed at which requests are processed, ensuring backend systems aren't overwhelmed by sudden request spikes.

Implementation Example: In Apigee, developers can define rate-limiting policies using a combination of quotas and spike arrest policies to prevent traffic surges from impacting backend systems.

3. Advanced Load Balancing Patterns

API gateways can distribute incoming requests across multiple instances of microservices to enhance reliability and scalability. Effective load balancing ensures even distribution of traffic and optimizes resource utilization across services.

Common Load Balancing Strategies:

- **Round-Robin**: Distributes incoming requests evenly across available instances.
- **Least Connections**: Routes traffic to the instance with the fewest active connections.
- **Weighted Load Balancing**: Allocates traffic based on predefined weights, allowing more powerful instances to handle a larger share of requests.
- **Geographical Load Balancing**: Routes requests based on client location, optimizing latency for users.

Implementation Example: In Azure API Management, developers can configure load balancing across multiple backend services using built-in policies and traffic distribution algorithms.

4. Protocol Translation for Hybrid Environments

API gateways often need to communicate with different services using various protocols, such as REST, gRPC, GraphQL, and SOAP. Protocol translation allows the gateway to act as a bridge between these protocols, enabling seamless integration between modern and legacy systems.

Common Scenarios for Protocol Translation:

- **REST to gRPC**: Converting RESTful API calls to gRPC for internal microservices communication, which can offer improved performance due to its compact binary protocol.
- **REST to GraphQL**: Enabling clients to request specific fields using GraphQL, while the gateway translates these requests into RESTful calls

to backend services.

- **SOAP to REST**: Providing a RESTful interface to modern clients while maintaining communication with legacy SOAP-based systems.

Implementation Example: AWS API Gateway supports integration with AWS AppSync for GraphQL or gRPC backends, allowing developers to create a RESTful entry point while leveraging advanced features of these protocols internally.

Monitoring and Observability

Effective monitoring and observability are vital for ensuring that API gateways perform optimally and reliably. They provide insights into system behavior, help detect anomalies, and facilitate proactive management of performance issues. Here's how you can implement comprehensive monitoring for your API gateway:

1. Setting Up API Metrics and Dashboards

Monitoring key performance indicators (KPIs) like latency, throughput, error rates, and resource utilization is essential for maintaining a healthy API gateway. These metrics allow you to identify potential issues early and optimize resource allocation.

Common Metrics to Monitor:

- **Request Latency**: Measures the time taken for requests to be processed, from receipt to response.
- **Error Rates**: Tracks the number of failed requests or responses with status codes like 4xx (client errors) and 5xx (server errors).
- **Request Count and Throughput**: Measures the volume of requests handled over time, providing insights into peak usage periods.
- **Backend Health**: Monitors the health of backend services, identifying bottlenecks or failures that could impact API performance.

Implementation Example: In Google Cloud Apigee, developers can use **Apigee Edge** to monitor API traffic, analyze request patterns, and view detailed metrics dashboards. Real-time dashboards provide visibility into API performance and allow teams to react to issues quickly.

2. Distributed Tracing for Service Dependencies

In microservices-based architectures, requests often pass through multiple services before a response is returned. Distributed tracing allows you to track the journey of each request across these services, identifying bottlenecks or points of failure.

Benefits of Distributed Tracing:

- **Improved Debugging**: Quickly locate problematic services or slow endpoints within complex service chains.
- **Performance Analysis**: Measure and analyze the time spent at each service, enabling more precise optimizations.
- **Dependency Visualization**: Visualize service dependencies and communication paths to understand the overall system architecture.

Implementation Example: Tools like **AWS X-Ray** can be integrated with AWS API Gateway and Lambda functions to trace requests from the gateway through each service. **Azure Application Insights** offers similar functionality for distributed tracing in Azure environments.

3. Automated Alerting and SLA Management

Automated alerting ensures that teams are promptly notified of critical issues, allowing them to take corrective actions before they impact end users. Setting up alerts for key metrics and establishing Service Level Agreements (SLAs) helps maintain reliability and trust.

Best Practices for Alerting:

- **Threshold-Based Alerts**: Set up alerts for specific thresholds, such as latency exceeding a certain limit or error rates crossing an acceptable range.
- **Anomaly Detection**: Use machine learning-based anomaly detection to identify unexpected deviations in traffic patterns or performance metrics.
- **SLA Enforcement**: Monitor compliance with SLAs, ensuring that

uptime and response time commitments are met consistently.

Implementation Example: In Azure API Management, **Azure Monitor** can be used to create custom alerts based on metrics like request success rates, latency, or server errors. Alerts can be configured to send notifications via email, SMS, or integrated tools like Slack or Microsoft Teams.

Security Enhancements and Compliance

API gateways play a critical role in enforcing security policies and ensuring compliance with industry standards. Security measures should be implemented at the gateway level to protect sensitive data, prevent unauthorized access, and mitigate threats.

1. Implementing Zero Trust at the Gateway Level

The **Zero Trust** security model is based on the principle of "never trust, always verify." API gateways play a vital role in implementing zero trust by continuously validating each request, regardless of its origin or the requester's network location.

Key Features of Zero Trust at API Gateways:

- **Identity Verification**: Enforce strong authentication mechanisms like OAuth2, multi-factor authentication (MFA), or SAML at the gateway level.
- **Continuous Authorization**: Validate JWT tokens and user permissions with each request to prevent unauthorized access.
- **Contextual Access Control**: Make access decisions based on contextual factors such as user roles, device security posture, or geographical location.

Implementation Example: Google Cloud Apigee provides built-in policies for identity verification and continuous authorization using OAuth2 and OpenID Connect (OIDC). It supports integrating external identity providers for enhanced security.

2. Data Encryption and Secure Traffic Management

29

Encryption of data in transit and at rest is crucial for protecting sensitive information. API gateways can enforce secure traffic management policies to ensure all communications are encrypted and follow compliance standards.

Best Practices for Data Encryption:

- **TLS Termination**: Enforce SSL/TLS encryption for all incoming and outgoing traffic at the gateway level. Terminating TLS at the gateway offloads decryption work from backend services.
- **End-to-End Encryption**: Extend encryption policies beyond the gateway to internal services, ensuring that sensitive data remains protected throughout its lifecycle.
- **Data Masking and Tokenization**: Implement data masking or tokenization policies at the gateway to protect sensitive information like credit card numbers or personally identifiable information (PII).

Implementation Example: In Azure API Management, you can enforce TLS for all incoming requests and configure secure backend connections to protect sensitive traffic between the gateway and backend services.

3. Compliance Requirements: GDPR, HIPAA, and Beyond

API gateways are instrumental in achieving compliance with industry regulations like **General Data Protection Regulation (GDPR)** and **Health Insurance Portability and Accountability Act (HIPAA)**. They help enforce policies related to data privacy, access controls, and monitoring.

Steps for Achieving Compliance:

- **Data Retention Policies**: Use API gateways to enforce data retention and deletion policies for sensitive information, aligning with GDPR requirements.
- **Audit Logging**: Maintain detailed audit logs of all API activities, including access attempts, modifications, and data exchanges, to ensure accountability.
- **Role-Based Access Control (RBAC)**: Enforce RBAC policies at the gateway level to limit access based on user roles and responsibilities.

Implementation Example: In AWS API Gateway, logging and monitoring capabilities can be combined with CloudTrail and AWS Config to provide a detailed audit trail for compliance purposes. Additionally, Lambda Authorizers can be used to enforce strict access controls.

Practical Applications and Advanced Topics

API gateways serve as essential building blocks in cloud-native architectures, connecting services and clients, enhancing security, and enabling seamless interactions. In this section, we'll explore practical applications and advanced topics that demonstrate how to leverage API gateways in various contexts. These include serverless API gateway patterns, hybrid cloud and multi-cloud architectures, and emerging technologies like GraphQL and gRPC. By mastering these concepts, readers will be equipped to implement API gateways that are not only functional but future-proof.

Serverless API Gateway Patterns

The rise of serverless computing has revolutionized cloud architecture by allowing developers to focus on code rather than infrastructure. API gateways play a critical role in serverless applications, providing a reliable and scalable entry point to serverless functions.

Event-Driven Architectures with API Gateways

Serverless architectures thrive on event-driven models, where different services are triggered by specific events like HTTP requests, changes in data, or system events. API gateways serve as the central point for processing and routing these events to serverless functions.

Example Scenario: A media-sharing application allows users to upload, process, and view images. The application is entirely serverless, leveraging

AWS Lambda functions and an API Gateway.

Architecture Flow:

1. **Image Upload**: Users upload images via an API exposed by the API Gateway. This triggers a Lambda function that processes the image (e.g., compresses or resizes it) and stores it in S3.
2. **Real-Time Notifications**: Upon successful image upload, an event is emitted to trigger a Lambda function that sends real-time notifications to subscribers.
3. **Image Retrieval**: When users request to view images, the API Gateway routes the request to another Lambda function that retrieves metadata and pre-signed URLs for S3 objects.

Managing Cold Starts and Scaling Serverless APIs

Serverless platforms, while offering scalability, come with challenges like cold starts—where functions are spun up from a cold state, leading to latency. API gateways help mitigate these challenges by offering:

- **Connection Reuse**: Maintaining persistent connections between the gateway and backend services, reducing the impact of cold starts.
- **API Caching**: Caching responses for frequently accessed APIs reduces the number of cold-start invocations for common requests.

Example Strategy: AWS API Gateway can be configured with **provisioned concurrency** for critical Lambda functions to ensure they are pre-warmed and ready to handle incoming traffic with minimal latency.

Multi-Cloud and Hybrid API Gateway Architectures

Enterprises are increasingly adopting multi-cloud and hybrid cloud strategies to avoid vendor lock-in and enhance resilience. API gateways must be capable of handling cross-cloud and on-premises integration scenarios while maintaining consistent security policies and performance standards.

Managing API Gateways Across Multiple Cloud Providers

A multi-cloud strategy involves deploying different services across multiple cloud providers, like AWS, Azure, and Google Cloud. An API gateway in this context serves as a unified entry point that abstracts the complexity of multi-cloud deployments from end-users.

Challenges in Multi-Cloud Environments:

- **Consistent Policy Enforcement**: Each cloud provider may have unique security policies and configurations, requiring the API gateway to enforce consistent policies regardless of the backend cloud provider.
- **Routing and Traffic Management**: The API gateway must be capable of intelligent traffic routing based on factors like service location, latency, and compliance requirements.
- **Cost Optimization**: Multi-cloud environments can result in increased costs if not managed properly. API gateways must facilitate efficient resource allocation and utilization.

Example Architecture: A financial services company utilizes AWS for compute-intensive tasks, Azure for data analytics, and Google Cloud for customer-facing APIs. A multi-cloud API gateway, such as **Apigee hybrid** or **Kong**, acts as a centralized management layer, directing traffic based on the most suitable cloud provider for each API.

Hybrid Cloud Integration with API Gateways

Hybrid cloud strategies involve connecting on-premises systems with cloud services, enabling organizations to leverage the benefits of both environments. API gateways facilitate this integration by securely bridging the two environments and centralizing policy management.

Example Scenario: A manufacturing company has legacy on-premises systems for inventory management and utilizes AWS for predictive analytics. An API gateway enables seamless integration by exposing on-premises inventory APIs alongside cloud-based analytics APIs.

Hybrid Integration Strategy:

1. **Secure API Exposure**: The API gateway exposes legacy APIs securely to the cloud environment, applying policies like SSL encryption, IP whitelisting, and request validation.
2. **Direct Data Transfer**: It facilitates direct data exchange between on-premises systems and cloud-based services while maintaining data integrity and compliance.
3. **Unified Monitoring**: A centralized monitoring setup provides a unified view of API traffic, performance, and health metrics across both on-premises and cloud environments.

Emerging Trends: GraphQL, gRPC, and Edge Computing

Modern API gateways are adapting to new paradigms in API design and architecture. As businesses seek more efficient and flexible communication models, protocols like GraphQL and gRPC are gaining popularity. Edge computing is also emerging as a key trend for reducing latency and enhancing real-time processing.

Implementing API Gateways for GraphQL

GraphQL offers a more flexible and efficient way of interacting with APIs by allowing clients to request only the data they need. While traditional REST APIs expose multiple endpoints, GraphQL exposes a single endpoint with a rich query language.

Integrating GraphQL with API Gateways:

- **Centralized Schema Management**: Use the API gateway to manage and validate GraphQL schemas, ensuring consistency across different services.
- **Schema Stitching**: For complex applications, API gateways can stitch multiple GraphQL schemas together, providing a unified interface for interacting with different services.
- **Rate Limiting and Security**: Implement rate limiting and security policies at the gateway level to prevent abuse of flexible queries.

Example Scenario: An eCommerce platform uses GraphQL to expose product details, user reviews, and recommendations. The API gateway provides centralized access to GraphQL queries and mutations while enforcing security and rate limits.

gRPC Integration and Streaming APIs

gRPC is a high-performance, open-source RPC framework that uses HTTP/2 for transport and Protobuf for message serialization. It provides strong typing, automatic code generation, and support for bi-directional streaming, making it an attractive choice for internal service-to-service communication.

API Gateway and gRPC:

- **Protocol Translation**: Use API gateways to expose gRPC services as RESTful APIs for external clients while maintaining gRPC-based internal communication.
- **Security and Authentication**: Apply centralized authentication and authorization policies at the API gateway level, regardless of whether the backend services use gRPC or REST.
- **Bi-Directional Streaming**: API gateways can serve as intermediaries for gRPC-based streaming APIs, enabling real-time interactions between clients and services.

Example Scenario: A video conferencing platform uses gRPC for real-time messaging between backend services. The API gateway translates gRPC messages to REST for external integrations, providing flexibility to external developers.

Leveraging Edge Gateways for Low Latency Applications

As applications require faster response times and localized processing, edge computing is emerging as a vital architectural trend. API gateways deployed at edge locations allow for low-latency interactions and efficient processing of data close to users.

Edge Gateway Architecture:

- **Proximity to Users**: Deploy API gateways at edge locations to reduce the latency of critical APIs and improve the user experience.
- **Edge Caching and Computation**: Implement caching strategies at the edge gateway to minimize the load on central servers and accelerate content delivery.
- **Real-Time Data Processing**: Use edge API gateways to perform real-time data processing, filtering, and transformation before forwarding data to central systems.

Example Scenario: A gaming platform deploys edge API gateways to provide real-time game state updates to players. Edge caching and localized processing ensure that users experience minimal latency and smooth gameplay.

Lesser-Known API Gateway Features and Techniques

Beyond the standard functionalities, API gateways often provide advanced features that can greatly enhance flexibility and efficiency. Exploring these lesser-known techniques can give you an edge in optimizing your gateway implementations.

1. API Monetization and Developer Portals

Monetizing APIs allows businesses to charge customers or partners for using specific APIs. Developer portals provide a centralized platform for publishing and managing APIs, offering features like documentation, API keys, and usage analytics.

Monetization Techniques:

- **Usage-Based Billing**: Charge users based on the number of API requests or the volume of data transferred.
- **Subscription Tiers**: Offer tiered access levels with different pricing models, such as free, standard, and premium plans.
- **Pay-As-You-Go**: Implement flexible pricing models that adapt to changing usage patterns and customer needs.

Developer Portals:

- **API Key Management**: Allow users to generate, manage, and revoke API keys securely.
- **Self-Service Onboarding**: Provide intuitive onboarding workflows with detailed API documentation and sample code.

Example Scenario: A cloud-based CRM platform exposes its APIs to third-party developers through a dedicated portal. API monetization allows the platform to charge partners based on their monthly API usage.

2. Dynamic API Routing and Service Mesh Integration

API gateways can integrate with service meshes like Istio, Linkerd, or Consul to enhance service-to-service communication. Service meshes provide fine-grained control over service-to-service interactions, offering advanced features like traffic splitting, fault injection, and circuit breaking.

Dynamic API Routing:

- **Intelligent Routing**: Route traffic based on dynamic factors such as real-time load, service availability, or client location.
- **A/B Testing and Canary Deployments**: API gateways can facilitate A/B testing by directing a portion of traffic to new service versions and gradually increasing the share based on performance.

Service Mesh Integration:

- **Policy Enforcement**: Implement centralized security, encryption, and logging policies across microservices using a combination of API gateways and service meshes.
- **Observability and Telemetry**: Leverage service mesh capabilities to gain detailed insights into service-to-service communication patterns and detect potential issues.

Example Scenario: A fintech company uses Istio as a service mesh for microservices communication. The API gateway acts as the external entry point, while Istio manages internal traffic routing, load balancing, and monitoring.

Hands-On Projects and Case Studies

A pplying the concepts learned in real-world scenarios is crucial to mastering API gateway design. This section provides a series of hands-on projects and case studies that demonstrate how to implement API gateways effectively. Each project highlights different use cases, from integrating serverless and microservices architectures to securing APIs in regulated industries. By working through these projects, readers can gain practical experience and insights into best practices for API gateway deployment and management.

Project 1: API Gateway for an eCommerce Platform

Scenario: You're building an eCommerce platform named *ShopFlow* that offers features like product browsing, order management, and payment processing. The architecture includes a combination of microservices and serverless functions. The goal of this project is to design and implement an API gateway that centralizes security, optimizes traffic routing, and enhances scalability.

Objectives:

- Implement centralized security policies with OAuth2 authentication.
- Design API routing strategies to manage product, order, and payment services.
- Use caching and rate limiting to optimize performance.

Step 1: Setting Up the Architecture

Overview of Services:

- **Product Service**: A microservice for managing the product catalog.
- **Order Service**: A serverless function for order processing.
- **Payment Service**: A microservice responsible for handling payments and transactions.

API Gateway Requirements:

- **Security**: Use Amazon Cognito to authenticate users with OAuth2 and JWT tokens.
- **Routing**: Configure the API gateway to route requests to the correct service based on the URL path.
- **Rate Limiting and Caching**: Implement rate limiting to control traffic spikes and caching for frequently accessed data.

Step 2: Creating the API Gateway

- **Define API Resources**:
- Create an API gateway named *ShopFlow API*.
- Set up paths for /products, /orders, and /payments to route requests to the respective backend services.
- **Configure OAuth2 Authentication**:
- Create a Cognito user pool and configure OAuth2 scopes for different access levels, such as read:products and write:orders.
- Set up an **authorizer** in the API gateway to validate JWT tokens issued by Cognito.
- **Enable Caching and Rate Limiting**:
- Enable caching at the endpoint level for /products to reduce latency for product browsing requests.
- Create a usage plan with a rate limit of 100 requests per second per user and a quota of 10,000 requests per month.

Step 3: Testing and Monitoring

- **Testing**: Simulate multiple user requests to test API routing, authentication, caching, and rate limiting.
- **Monitoring**: Set up CloudWatch metrics to track latency, error rates, and throughput. Use alerts to notify the team of critical issues.

Outcome and Benefits:

This project provides a scalable and secure architecture for an eCommerce platform, leveraging API gateway features to centralize authentication, caching, and traffic management.

Project 2: Migrating a Legacy System with the Strangler Fig Pattern

Scenario: You're working for a logistics company that wants to migrate its monolithic legacy system to a microservices-based architecture. The goal is to implement the **Strangler Fig Pattern** to gradually replace legacy components with new microservices using an API gateway.

Objectives:

- Implement a central API gateway to route traffic between legacy and new microservices.
- Gradually migrate features from the monolithic system to new microservices.
- Maintain seamless client interactions throughout the migration.

Step 1: Planning the Migration

Legacy Features:

- **Order Management**: Handled by the legacy system.
- **Route Optimization**: To be implemented as a new microservice.

API Gateway Strategy:

- Set up an API gateway to handle traffic for /orders and /routes.
- Route /orders traffic to the legacy system initially.
- Implement the new route optimization microservice and gradually switch the routing logic in the API gateway.

Step 2: Implementing the API Gateway

- **Configure Routing for Legacy APIs**:
- Create an API named *Logistics API Gateway*.
- Define paths for /orders to route traffic to the existing legacy system's endpoints.
- **Introduce the Route Optimization Microservice**:
- Develop the route optimization service and deploy it as a separate microservice.
- Update the API gateway configuration to route /routes traffic to the new microservice.
- **Switch Legacy Routing Gradually**:
- As new features are implemented, update the routing rules in the API gateway to direct relevant traffic to the new microservices instead of the legacy system.

Outcome and Benefits:

This project demonstrates how to use the Strangler Fig Pattern to migrate a monolithic application incrementally. By leveraging an API gateway, the migration is seamless, with minimal disruptions to users.

Project 3: Multi-Cloud API Gateway for a Global SaaS Provider

Scenario: You're designing a multi-cloud architecture for a global SaaS provider that serves clients in different regions. The company uses AWS, Azure, and Google Cloud for different parts of its infrastructure. The objective is to create an API gateway that efficiently routes traffic across these clouds and enforces consistent policies.

Objectives:

- Design a multi-cloud API gateway that supports AWS, Azure, and Google Cloud backends.
- Implement intelligent traffic routing based on geographical proximity and service health.
- Enforce centralized security and monitoring policies.

Step 1: Designing the Multi-Cloud Architecture
Cloud Providers and Services:

- **AWS**: Handles compute-intensive tasks.
- **Azure**: Manages data analytics services.
- **Google Cloud**: Exposes customer-facing APIs.

API Gateway Strategy:

- Use a multi-cloud API gateway (such as Kong or Apigee hybrid) to act as a unified entry point for clients.
- Implement traffic routing logic based on factors like geographical location, latency, and service health.

Step 2: Implementing Cross-Cloud Traffic Routing

- **Configure Cross-Cloud Routing**:
- Define rules in the API gateway to route traffic based on the nearest cloud region for users. For example, route clients in Europe to Azure services, while routing clients in the US to AWS.
- **Centralize Security Policies**:
- Implement consistent security policies across all clouds, including authentication, encryption, and request validation.
- **Set Up Unified Monitoring**:
- Use integrated monitoring tools like **Prometheus** or **Grafana** to collect metrics from all cloud services and visualize them in a single dashboard.

Outcome and Benefits:

This project illustrates how to implement a multi-cloud architecture using an API gateway, achieving a balance between regional performance, centralized security, and unified monitoring.

Project 4: Securing APIs in a Regulated Industry (Healthcare)

Scenario: You're working on a healthcare application that handles sensitive patient data and needs to comply with strict regulations like **HIPAA**. The goal of this project is to secure APIs using an API gateway and implement monitoring for regulatory compliance.

Objectives:

- Implement OAuth2 authentication and enforce strict access controls.
- Set up detailed logging and auditing for compliance purposes.
- Ensure end-to-end encryption of sensitive data.

Step 1: Designing the Secure API Gateway

Security Requirements:

- **Authentication and Authorization**: Enforce OAuth2 and JWT-based access controls for all APIs.
- **Audit Logging**: Maintain detailed logs of all API activities, including access attempts and data modifications.
- **Data Encryption**: Use TLS to encrypt data in transit and ensure secure backend communications.

API Gateway Strategy:

- Use **Apigee** or **Azure API Management** to implement OAuth2 authentication and centralized security policies.
- Configure audit logging and integrate with external monitoring tools for detailed reporting.

Step 2: Implementing Security and Compliance Policies

- **Set Up OAuth2 Authentication**:
- Create an authorization server and define OAuth2 scopes for accessing patient data (e.g., read:patient_records and write:patient_notes).
- Configure JWT validation policies at the gateway level.
- **Enable Audit Logging and Alerts**:
- Set up detailed logging of all API activities and store logs securely in a centralized repository.
- Define alerts for suspicious activities, such as repeated unauthorized access attempts or unusual data access patterns.
- **Implement End-to-End Encryption**:
- Enforce TLS encryption for all incoming and outgoing traffic.
- Apply data masking or tokenization policies to protect sensitive information.

Outcome and Benefits:

This project showcases the importance of securing APIs in regulated industries like healthcare. By implementing strong authentication, detailed logging, and end-to-end encryption, the API gateway helps ensure regulatory compliance.

Case Study 1: Building an Edge API Gateway for a Gaming Platform

Scenario: A gaming company wants to deploy an API gateway at edge locations to improve response times for real-time multiplayer games. The goal is to design an edge API gateway that optimizes latency and provides real-time updates.

Objectives:

- Deploy edge API gateways close to users to reduce latency.
- Implement caching strategies for frequently accessed game data.
- Use real-time streaming to push game state updates to players.

Strategy and Implementation:

- **Deploy Edge API Gateways:**
- Deploy API gateways at strategic edge locations using a content delivery network (CDN) like **AWS CloudFront** or **Azure Front Door**.
- Route client requests to the nearest edge location based on proximity.
- **Optimize Latency with Edge Caching:**
- Cache frequently accessed game data at edge locations, reducing the need to query central servers.
- Implement cache invalidation policies to ensure real-time accuracy.
- **Use WebSocket APIs for Real-Time Updates:**
- Enable WebSocket APIs at the edge API gateway to push real-time game state updates to players, ensuring a smooth gaming experience.

Outcome and Benefits:

This case study highlights the benefits of deploying edge API gateways for low-latency applications like gaming. By strategically caching data and using real-time APIs, the gaming platform achieves improved performance and responsiveness.

Case Study 2: Implementing GraphQL APIs for a Fintech Company

Scenario: A fintech company wants to use GraphQL to expose financial data APIs while enforcing strict security and access controls. The goal is to design an API gateway that integrates with GraphQL and enforces centralized policies.

Objectives:

- Implement GraphQL with an API gateway to offer flexible data queries.
- Secure GraphQL APIs with authentication and rate limiting.
- Monitor GraphQL usage and performance.

Strategy and Implementation:

- **Expose GraphQL APIs**:
- Set up a GraphQL server and integrate it with the API gateway, exposing a unified endpoint for financial data queries.
- **Enforce Security Policies**:
- Implement JWT-based authentication to control access to sensitive financial data.
- Apply rate-limiting policies to prevent abuse of flexible GraphQL queries.
- **Monitor GraphQL Traffic**:
- Use monitoring tools to track query patterns, response times, and errors.
- Implement analytics to gain insights into API usage and client behavior.

Outcome and Benefits:

This case study demonstrates how to integrate GraphQL with an API gateway, providing flexible and secure APIs for a fintech company. By centralizing security and monitoring, the company ensures that sensitive data remains protected.

Advanced Best Practices and Future Directions

API gateways are more than just gateways to services; they are critical architectural components that can greatly influence the performance, security, and scalability of cloud-native applications. This section covers advanced best practices that enhance the efficiency and robustness of API gateways. We will also explore future trends and innovations that will shape the evolution of API gateways in the years to come. By understanding these advanced strategies and keeping an eye on emerging developments, you will be well-equipped to design resilient and forward-looking API gateway implementations.

Advanced Best Practices

API gateways need to be optimized to handle complex requirements, evolving security threats, and diverse communication protocols. Here are some advanced best practices to ensure optimal performance and security:

1. Implementing Blue-Green and Canary Deployments

Deployment strategies like **Blue-Green** and **Canary Deployments** are essential for reducing the risk of deploying new features or updates. API gateways can be configured to facilitate these deployment models, minimizing downtime and allowing seamless version rollouts.

- **Blue-Green Deployment**: In this strategy, two identical production environments (Blue and Green) are maintained. API gateways route traffic to the active environment (e.g., Blue). When deploying a new version, the Green environment is updated and tested. If all tests pass, traffic is switched to Green. This approach minimizes downtime and provides a quick rollback mechanism.

- **Canary Deployment**: API gateways allow routing a small percentage of traffic to the updated version (Canary) while the majority of users remain on the stable version. This technique is ideal for monitoring new releases in a real-world environment without exposing all users to potential issues.

Best Practice: Use API gateways like **AWS API Gateway, Azure API Management,** or **Kong** to manage version routing and automate traffic switching. Configure routing policies that direct a specific percentage of traffic to the Canary version and gradually increase this percentage as the new version proves stable.

2. Securing APIs with Mutual TLS and Advanced Authentication Mechanisms

API gateways are at the forefront of handling and enforcing security policies. For applications that require strict security measures, implementing **Mutual TLS (mTLS)** and advanced authentication mechanisms can provide an additional layer of protection.

- **Mutual TLS**: Unlike standard TLS, where only the client authenticates the server, mutual TLS requires both client and server to authenticate each other using certificates. This approach prevents unauthorized clients from connecting to APIs.
- **Advanced Authentication**: While OAuth2 and JWT are commonly used, combining them with **SAML** (Security Assertion Markup Language) for federated authentication in enterprise environments or implementing **certificate-based authentication** for machine-to-machine (M2M) communication can further strengthen security.

Best Practice: Configure API gateways to enforce mutual TLS for sensitive APIs and use external identity providers to validate certificates. Combine OAuth2 with additional factors like **FIDO2** tokens or biometric authentication for enhanced user identity verification.

3. Automating Configuration Management with Infrastructure as Code (IaC)

To maintain consistency and efficiency, automate the deployment and configuration of API gateways using Infrastructure as Code (IaC) tools like **Terraform, AWS CloudFormation,** or **Azure Resource Manager**. This approach ensures that API gateway configurations are versioned, repeatable, and easy to deploy across environments.

- **Versioned Configuration**: Store API gateway configurations in a version control system (VCS) like **Git** to track changes and facilitate collaboration.
- **Automated CI/CD Pipelines**: Integrate IaC with continuous integration and deployment pipelines to automate the testing and deployment of API gateway updates.

Best Practice: Use Terraform modules or CloudFormation templates to define API gateway configurations, security policies, and routing rules. Incorporate automated testing for API gateways as part of your CI/CD pipeline to ensure that any changes do not introduce unintended issues.

4. Leveraging Centralized Logging and Distributed Tracing

Centralized logging and distributed tracing provide deep visibility into API gateway interactions and backend service performance. They help detect bottlenecks, identify errors, and understand the flow of requests through complex architectures.

- **Centralized Logging**: Implement centralized logging solutions like **ELK Stack (Elasticsearch, Logstash, Kibana), Splunk,** or **Azure Monitor**

51

to aggregate and analyze logs from API gateways and backend services.

- **Distributed Tracing**: Use tracing tools like **AWS X-Ray**, **Jaeger**, or **OpenTelemetry** to trace requests from the API gateway through each microservice. This enables you to pinpoint performance issues and optimize service interactions.

Best Practice: Set up logging policies at the API gateway level to capture essential metrics like request latency, status codes, and error messages. Implement tracing headers for all requests passing through the gateway to facilitate end-to-end observability.

5. Embracing Policy as Code for Consistent Policy Enforcement

As applications grow more complex, ensuring consistent security, compliance, and governance policies becomes challenging. The concept of **Policy as Code** enables teams to define policies programmatically and enforce them across API gateways and services.

- **Define Policies Programmatically**: Use policy-as-code frameworks like **Open Policy Agent (OPA)** to define access control, rate limiting, and logging policies as code. Store these policies in a version control system to track changes.
- **Automated Policy Validation**: Integrate policy checks into CI/CD pipelines to automatically validate policy compliance before deploying updates.

Best Practice: Adopt a unified policy framework like OPA to enforce consistent security and compliance policies across API gateways and microservices. Combine policy-as-code with automated testing to validate that policies are applied correctly in all environments.

Future Directions for API Gateways

API gateways are evolving rapidly to keep up with advancements in cloud computing, security, and developer requirements. Understanding these trends and their implications will help you design future-proof architectures and adopt new features as they become mainstream.

1. AI-Powered API Gateways and Intelligent Routing

As machine learning becomes more integrated with infrastructure, the concept of **AI-powered API gateways** is gaining traction. AI can help automate traffic routing, detect anomalies, and optimize performance.

- **Intelligent Traffic Routing**: AI-powered gateways can analyze historical traffic patterns and use predictive models to route requests dynamically based on factors like expected latency, load, and backend performance.
- **Anomaly Detection**: Machine learning algorithms can monitor API traffic and detect unusual activity patterns that could indicate DDoS attacks or misuse of APIs.

Future Trend: Cloud providers like **Google Cloud** and open-source projects are experimenting with AI models integrated into API management solutions. Expect to see more automation and self-optimization features in the next generation of API gateways.

2. Serverless and Edge API Gateways for Decentralized Architectures

The continued rise of **serverless computing** and **edge computing** is pushing API gateways to the edge of networks, enabling faster responses and localized processing. This trend allows applications to be more responsive and scalable.

- **Edge API Gateways**: Deployed at CDN edge locations, these gateways reduce latency by bringing APIs closer to end-users. They are ideal for applications requiring real-time data processing, such as IoT devices and gaming platforms.
- **Serverless API Gateways**: Serverless models are evolving to offer more granular control over traffic routing, caching, and request transforma-

tions without needing to manage infrastructure directly.

Future Trend: Look for API gateways that natively integrate with edge networks and serverless platforms, providing advanced features like local caching, in-memory data processing, and low-latency routing.

3. Expanding API Management to Support Mesh Architectures

Service meshes have emerged as a powerful way to manage microservices communication. As service mesh adoption grows, API gateways will need to integrate more deeply with these architectures to facilitate complex traffic routing and security policies.

- **Service Mesh Integration**: API gateways are increasingly being used in conjunction with service meshes like **Istio, Linkerd**, and **Consul**. This integration enables seamless management of traffic between services while maintaining observability and policy enforcement.
- **Advanced Traffic Shaping**: By integrating with service meshes, API gateways can perform more granular traffic shaping, including circuit breaking, retries, and per-request policy enforcement.

Future Trend: Service mesh and API gateway functionalities are converging, with open-source projects and cloud providers exploring ways to unify traffic management under a single architecture.

4. API-First Development and the Rise of Developer Portals

The growing emphasis on **API-first development** is changing how organizations design and expose APIs. Developer portals are becoming central hubs for collaboration, onboarding, and monetization of APIs.

- **API Productization**: APIs are increasingly treated as products, with dedicated developer portals providing detailed documentation, API keys, pricing plans, and analytics dashboards.
- **Self-Service API Publishing**: API gateways are enabling self-service

capabilities, allowing developers to design, deploy, and manage their own APIs without direct intervention from central IT teams.

Future Trend: Expect to see more comprehensive developer portals with built-in support for API testing, SDK generation, and usage analytics, simplifying the process of exposing APIs to external developers.

5. Enhanced Security and Zero Trust Architectures

As organizations adopt **Zero Trust** security models, API gateways are becoming central to enforcing zero trust principles. This approach focuses on continuous verification and fine-grained access controls for every request.

- **Continuous Authentication**: API gateways are evolving to support continuous authentication models that validate user identities, device postures, and session integrity in real-time.
- **Micro-Segmentation**: Enhanced API gateways are being integrated with network segmentation solutions to isolate services and enforce strict access policies based on dynamic factors.

Future Trend: Zero trust architectures will drive new innovations in API gateway security, with more emphasis on real-time monitoring, adaptive policies, and machine learning-driven threat detection.

55